Explore new ideas!

Welcome to your
California
Reading/Writing
Workshop

Read exciting science and social studies texts!

Become an expert writer!

Build vocabulary and knowledge to unlock the Wonders of reading!

Use your student login to explore your interactive Reading/Writing Workshop, practice close reading, and more.

Go Digital!   www.connected.mcgraw-hill.com

Cover and Title pages: Nathan Love

www.mheonline.com/readingwonders

ISBN: 978-0-02-130524-7
MHID: 0-02-130524-2

Printed in the United States of America.

2 3 4 5 6 7 8 9 DOW 20 19 18 17 16

B

Wonders

An English Language Arts Program

Program Authors

Diane August

Donald R. Bear

Janice A. Dole

Jana Echevarria

Douglas Fisher

David Francis

Vicki Gibson

Jan Hasbrouck

Margaret Kilgo

Jay McTighe

Scott G. Paris

Timothy Shanahan

Josefina V. Tinajero

Mc
Graw
Hill
Education

Unit 3

Changes Over Time

The Big Idea

What can happen over time? 6

SOCIAL STUDIES

Week 1 · What Time Is It?   8

SCIENCE

Week 2 · Watch It Grow!   28

(t) Cathy Delanssay; (c) Kenneth Spengler; (b) Dan Andreasen

Go Digital! Find all lessons online at: www.connected.mcgraw-hill.com.

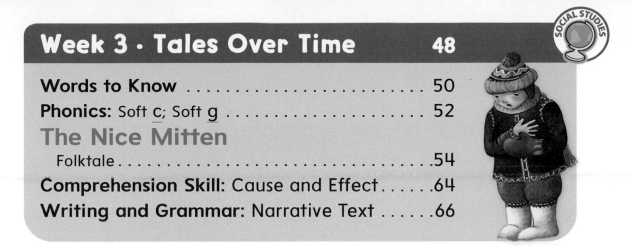
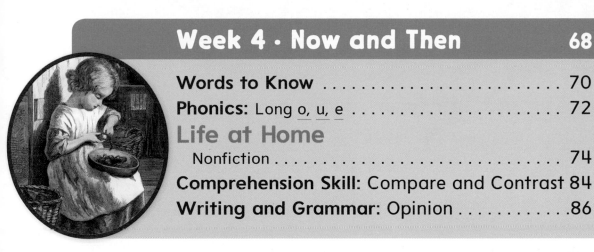
(t) Anna Vojtech; (c) North Wind/North Wind Picture Archives;
(b) Tanya Constantine/Blend Images/Getty Images

5

The Big Idea

What can happen over time?

Changes Over Time

Changes, Changes

Little by little, day by day,
Things grow and change in
every way.

Trees get taller and touch the sky,
Eggs hatch new birds who
learn to fly.

A puppy born in spring is small,
But he'll be bigger when it's fall.

I'm also growing, bit by bit,
Just see—my clothes no
longer fit!

—by George Samos

Cathy Delanssay

Essential Question

How do we measure time?

Go Digital!

COLLABORATE

Talk About It

What are these children learning to do?

Ariel Skelley/Blend Images/Corbis

8

All About Time

away

Do all birds fly **away** in fall?

now

It's time for us to eat **now**.

some

Some kids like to wear a watch.

today

It is my birthday **today**!

way

A clock is one **way** to tell time.

why

Why is summer a fun season?

Your Turn

Say the sentence for each word. Then make up another sentence.

Go Digital! *Use the online visual glossary*

(tl) Sean Duan/Flickr/Getty Images; (cl) BlueMoon Stock/Alamy; (bl) Shiyna Thenabadu/Alamy; (tr) UpperCut Images/Alamy; (cr) Comstock Images; (br) Fuse/Getty Images

Long a

The a_e spelling makes the long a sound in **wake**.

date	**whale**	**shakes**
wave	**safe**	**plate**
snake	**game**	**grapes**
trades	**vase**	**brave**

Kenneth Spengler

RF.1.3c, RF.1.3f See the California Standards section.

Dave gave Jane a plate of grapes.

Can the ants take the grapes?

Your Turn

Look for these words with long a spelled a_e in "Nate the Snake Is Late."

Nate   snake   late   make

wade   lake   wake   gaze

lane   gate   Tate

Essential Question

How do we measure time?

Read about how Nate the snake keeps track of time.

Go Digital!

Kenneth Spengler

14

Nate the Snake Is Late

It is 8 o'clock, and I can not be late.

I do not wish to make my pals wait.

I must be there at half past ten.

But I have lots of time until then.

Kenneth Spengler

At last I am set and on my **way** there,

But I think I still have **some** time to spare.

I wade in this lake as frogs
hop **away**.

I do not think they wish to play!

The sun is hot, and I nap on a rock.

Then I wake up and gaze at the clock.

Kenneth Spengler

Drats! It is 10 o'clock. Can it be?

Will my pals still be there for me?

I dash up a lane and past the gate.

I am on my way, but am I late?

My six best pals sit with Miss Tate.

I tell them all **why** I am late.

They grin at me and then they say,
"**Now** we can hear the story **today**!"

Character, Setting, Plot

A **character** is a person or an animal in a story. The **setting** is where and when a story takes place.

The **plot** of a story is what happens at the beginning, middle, and end.

🔍 Find Text Evidence

Find out what happens at the beginning of the story.

page 16

It is 8 o'clock, and I can not be late.

I do not wish to make my pals wait.

Beginning

Nate wakes up at 8 o'clock.
He does not want to be late.

Middle

Nate does many things, such as wade in the lake. Then he takes a nap.

End

Nate gets to the library late for story hour. But his friends wait for him.

Your Turn COLLABORATE

Talk about the plot of "Nate the Snake Is Late."

Go Digital! *Use the interactive graphic organizer*

Write About the Text

Pages 14–23

Luke

I responded to the prompt: **Add two pages between pages 17–18. What does Nate do to get ready?**

Student Model: *Narrative Text*

I have time to grab something to eat. A juicy, red apple is a yummy treat!

Grammar

The word **grab** is a **verb**, or action word.

Sensory Details

I used the words **juicy** and **red** to tell about the apple.

Polka Dot/Getty Images Plus/Getty Images

W.1.3, L.1.1e, L.1.1f See the California Standards section.

I need my cap.

Oh, where could it be?

I look by my bed.

There it is, I see! ◀——————

Rhyming Words

I ended my lines with the words <u>be</u> and <u>see</u>.

Your Turn

COLLABORATE

Add two pages to "Nate the Snake Is Late" telling what happens next. Write rhyming sentences like the story.

Go Digital!
Write your response online.
Use your editing checklist.

Weekly Concept Watch It Grow!

 Essential Question

How do plants change as they grow?

 *Go Digital!*

(bkgd) Masterfile; (inset) Jonathan Kitchen/Photographer's Choice RF/Getty Images

 Talk About It

What does the boy see growing? How will it change?

28

Ready, Set, Grow!

green

Peas and beans are **green**.

grow

Plants get big when they **grow**.

pretty

The flowers are **pretty** colors.

should

Which seeds **should** I plant?

together

Together we can pull the weeds.

water

Water comes out of the hose.

Your Turn

COLLABORATE

Say the sentence for each word. Then make up another sentence.

Go Digital! Use the online visual glossary

(tl) Goodah:ot/Alamy; (cl) Image Source/Alamy; (bl) FogSock/Alamy; (tr) Pixtal/age fotostock; (cr) Ariel Skalley/Blend Images/Getty Images; (br) Huntstock/The Agency Collection/Getty Images

Long i

The i_e spelling makes the long i sound, as in **bite**.

likes	white	five
whines	wide	size
ripe	hide	time
drives	prize	shine

Dan Andreasen

RF.1.3c, RF.1.3f See the California Standards section.

Five fine pumpkins are on a vine.

What size is the prize pumpkin?

Your Turn

Look for these words with long i spelled i_e in "Time to Plant!"

time	Mike	White	fine	five
shines	vines	like	while	
bite	ripe	piles	yikes	

Essential Question

How do plants change as they grow?

Read about how vegetable plants grow.

Go Digital!

Dan Andreasen

Time to Plant!

Cast

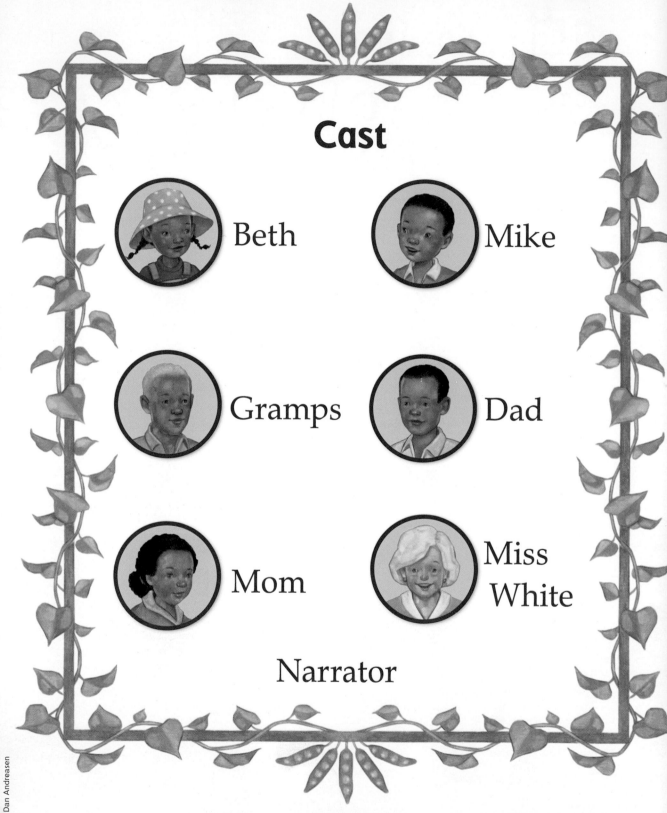

Beth

Mike

Gramps

Dad

Mom

Miss White

Narrator

Beth: Dad, can we plant a garden?

Dad: Yes! That will be fine!

Gramps: We can plant vegetables.

Mike: Yum! Let's do it **together**.

Mom: Dad and I will dig.

Mike: I will drop in five seeds.

Gramps: I will set in **green** plants.

Beth: And I will get **water**!

Dan Andreasen

Narrator: Days pass. The sun shines. Rain plinks and plunks.

Beth: I can spot buds on the vines!

Dad: Sun and water made them **grow**.

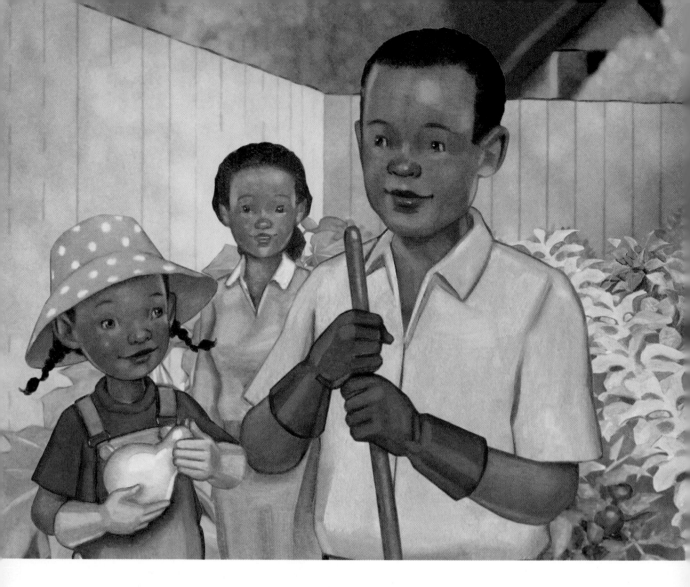

Narrator: Days pass. The sun shines. Rain drips and drops.

Beth: The vegetables got big!

Dad: We **should** pick them.

Mom: Yes, it's time!

Mike: I like to munch while I pick.
I will take a bite. Yum!

Gramps: Sun and water made
them ripe.

Narrator: They pick piles and piles.

Beth: Yikes! That's a lot!

Mike: We can't eat them all.

Gramps: I think I have a plan.

Dan Andreasen

Mike: This bag is for you.

Miss White: They are such **pretty** vegetables! Thank you!

Beth: Sun and water made them grow.

Sequence

Events in a story or a play happen in a certain order, or **sequence**. The events are the plot of the story.

 Find Text Evidence

Find the first thing that happens in "Time to Plant!"

page 37

> **Beth:** Dad, can we plant a garden?
>
> **Dad:** Yes! That will be fine!

Gramps: We can plant vegetables.

Mike: Yum! Let's do it **together**.

Dan Andreasen

First

The family plants a garden.

Next

The plants get big and grow.

Then

The family picks the vegetables.

Last

They share their vegetables.

COLLABORATE

Your Turn

Talk about the plot of "Time to Plant!"

Go Digital! Use the Interactive graphic organizer

45

Writing and Grammar

Pages 34–43

Write About the Text

Elizabeth

I responded to the prompt: **Write more lines for the end of the play. Tell what Miss White says.**

Student Model: *Narrative Text*

Miss White: Thank you! These vegetables look ripe and delicious. Will all of you join me for dinner? I can use the tomatoes to make a special soup.

Character
I wrote Miss White's name to tell the words that she says.

Specific Words
I used specific words, such as <u>tomatoes</u> instead of <u>vegetables</u>.

46

W.1.3 See the California Standards section.

Then I can slice the beans for a fine dish. I can add some fresh peas to our plates! I like fresh peas. It is fun to share a meal with friends!

Grammar

The **verb** like is in the present tense.

Your Turn

COLLABORATE

Add a page to the end of the story in which the kids tell Miss White what they did to grow the plants.

Go Digital!
Write your response online.
Use your editing checklist.

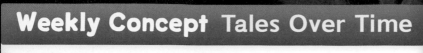

Essential Question

What is a folktale?

Go Digital!

Adam Taylor/Digital Vision/Getty Images

See the California Standards section.

Story Time

Talk About It

What are these children acting out?

49

any

Do you have **any** fairy tales?

from

Gram read to us **from** her book.

happy

I am **happy** to be in the play.

once

Once upon a time there was a queen.

so

That story is **so** funny!

upon

Once **upon** a time there was a king.

COLLABORATE

Your Turn

Say the sentence for each word. Then make up another sentence.

Go Digital! Use the online visual glossary

Soft c and Soft g

The letter c can make the soft c sound you hear in **race**.

The letters g and dge can make the soft g sound you hear in **age** and **edge**.

face	place	space
nice	slices	cents
page	cage	stage
pledge	fudge	gem

Anna Vojtech

52 RF.1.3b, RF.1.3f See the California Standards section.

Madge eats a big slice of fudge.

Gen likes to sing on a stage.

Your Turn

Look for these words with soft c and soft g in "The Nice Mitten."

nice	Lance	edge
mice	place	raced
hedgehog	space	trace

Essential Question

What is a folktale?

Read the story of a little boy's lost mitten.

Go Digital!

Anna Vojtech

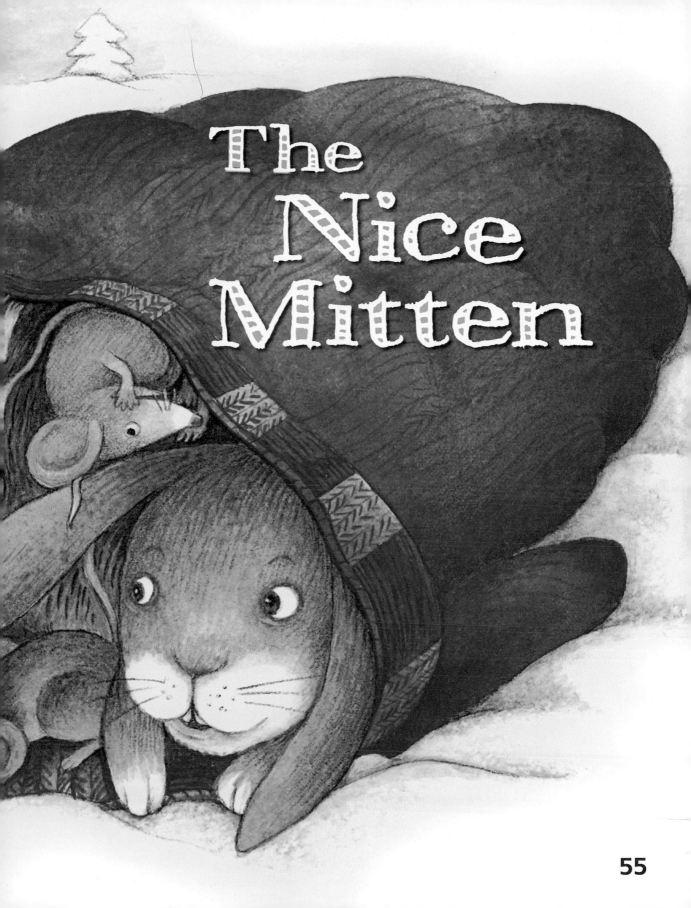

The Nice Mitten

Anna Vojtech

Once upon a time, a boy named Lance went out to pick up sticks. His mom gave him nice red mittens in case his hands got cold.

56

"Take the mittens and keep them safe," his mom said. But as Lance left, he ran fast and lost a mitten at the edge of the wide forest.

Five mice saw the mitten. "This is a nice place to rest," they said. **So** the **happy** mice went in and rested.

Then, a rabbit raced by. "This is
a nice place for hiding," she said.
So the rabbit went in and hid.
The mitten puffed up a bit.

Next, a hedgehog came sniffing
by. "This is a nice place for taking
a nap," he said. So the hedgehog
went in and slept. The mitten
puffed up a bit more.

Just then, a big bear came by. "This is a nice place to get warm," he said. So the big bear went in. The mitten puffed up **from** all the animals in it. It puffed up as much as a mitten can.

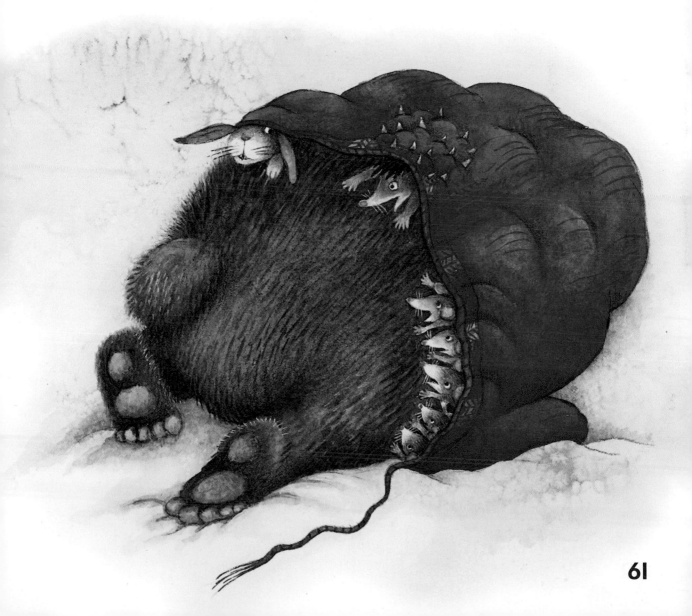

At last, a black cricket came by. "This is a nice place," he said.

"We do not have **any** space," said the animals in the mitten.

But the black cricket went in. And just as he did...

Rip! Snap! POP!

When Lance came back, there was not a trace of red mitten left. So sad!

Cause and Effect

A **cause** is what makes something happen in a story.

An **effect** is the event that happens.

To find the cause and the effect, ask: What happened? Why did it happen?

🔍 Find Text Evidence

Find the causes and effects in the story.

page 57

"Take the mittens and keep them safe," his mom said. But as Lance left, he ran fast and lost a mitten at the edge of the wide forest.

Anna Vojtech

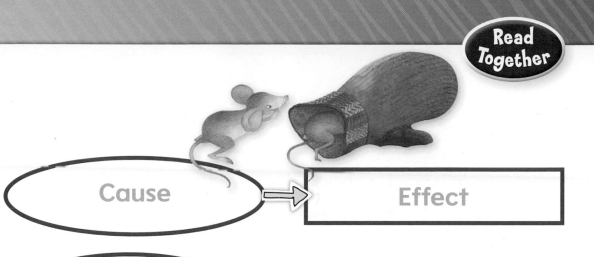

Cause		Effect
	→	
Lance ran fast.	→	He lost his mitten in the forest.
The animals wanted to rest.	→	The animals went inside the mitten.
Too many animals went in.	→	The mitten puffed up and got too big.

COLLABORATE

Your Turn

Talk about the cause and effect of story events in "The Nice Mitten."

Go Digital! *Use the interactive graphic organizer*

Write About the Text

Pages 54–63

Anna

I responded to the prompt: **Rewrite the story with a lost boot instead of a lost mitten.**

Student Model: *Narrative Text*

Once upon a time, Lance hiked to the river for water. On the way, he lost his boot in the sticky mud.

A wet mouse hid in his boot to dry off. Then, a bird flew in. Next, a fox crawled inside.

Strong Verbs

I used **strong verbs** such as <u>hiked</u>, <u>flew</u>, and <u>crawled</u> to make the story exciting.

Sequence

I told events in a sequence that made sense.

Sam74100/iStock/Getty Images Plus/Getty Images

Lance came back from the river. He found his boot in the mud. He shook it out, and all of the animals fell out.

The animals followed Lance home, and they all lived happily ever after.

Grammar

Verb endings like **-ed** tell about action in the **past.**

COLLABORATE

Your Turn

Rewrite the story so that the boy loses a jacket, sock, or hat instead of a mitten.

Go Digital!
Write your response online.
Use your editing checklist.

Essential Question

How is life different than it was long ago?

Go Digital!

SL.1.1a See the California Standards section.

Fox Photos/Hulton Archive/Getty Images

Once Upon a Time

COLLABORATE

Talk About It

What are the children playing? Tell how they are like or different than you.

ago

Schools were small long **ago**.

boy

That **boy** likes to skate.

girl

This **girl** can ride a bike well.

how

How did kids play in the past?

old

Old homes were made of logs.

people

People went by horse and buggy.

COLLABORATE

Your Turn

Say the sentence for each word. Then make up another sentence.

Go Digital! *Use the online visual glossary*

Long o, u, e

The o_e spelling makes the long o sound in **phone**.

The u_e spelling makes the long u sound in **use**.

The e_e spelling makes the long e sound in **these**.

bone	cute	Eve
drove	hoped	these
Steve	mule	stone
broke	voted	cubes

Valeria Cis

Can Pete use this phone?

Zeke is Rose's cute mule.

Your Turn

COLLABORATE

Look for these words with o_e, u_e, and e_e in "Life at Home."

home	homes	pole
huge	use	stove
these	those	

Essential Question

How is life different than it was long ago?

Read about how life at home is different today than it was long ago.

Go Digital!

Life at Home

Has home life changed a lot since long **ago**?

Yes, it has!

Long ago, many families cooked worked, and slept in one room.

Today, families can live in large homes that have lots of space.

A long time ago, homes had just one room. **People** ate and slept in that same room.

Today, homes can have many rooms.

Panorama Productions/Alamy

How did people cook and bake long ago?

A home had a brick fireplace with a pole. A huge pot hung on this pole. People cooked in this big pot.

Long ago, there was an oven at the side of the fireplace. Bread was baked there.

Today, stoves can use gas or electricity.

Now, we use a stove
to cook and bake things.
We still use pots.
But these pots are not
as big as that **old** pot!

Back then, kids helped out a lot.
A **boy** helped his dad plant crops.
A **girl** helped her mom inside the
home. She made socks and caps.
It takes a long time to make those
things.

A spinning wheel was used
to spin wool into yarn.

Today, people buy most of the things they need and want.

Now, we shop for things such as socks and caps. We shop for things to eat, as well.

But kids still help out at home.

Back then, people got water from a well. Then they filled up a big tub and washed things.

In the past, people washed dishes in a tub made of wood.

Now, people can wash things in a sink. We can wash dishes in a dishwasher, too.

Life is not as hard today as it was long ago!

Today, it's easy to wash dishes in a sink or dishwasher.

Jose Luis Pelaez/Blend Images/age fotostock

Compare and Contrast

When you compare, you think about how things are alike.

When you contrast, you think about how things are different.

🔍 Find Text Evidence

Find out how homes long ago and today are alike and different.

page 77

A long time ago, homes had just one room. **People** ate and slept in that same room.

Today, homes can have many rooms.

Panorama Productions/Alamy

RI.1.3 See the California Standards section.

Long Ago
Homes had one room.

Both
People live in homes.

Now
Homes have many rooms.

COLLABORATE

Your Turn

Talk about how home life is alike and different in "Life at Home."

Go Digital! *Use the interactive graphic organizer*

Pages 74–83

Write About the Text

I answered the question: **Would you rather cook as we do now or as people did long ago? Why?**

Mateo

Topic

I named the selection and what I wrote about.

Reasons

I gave a reason for my opinion.

Student Model: *Opinion*

I read "Life at Home" and I would rather cook as we do now. Long ago, people cooked over a big fire. They used one big pot. They could only make one thing at a time.

Now we use a stove to cook. We can cook many things because the stove is able to fit many pots. I like that cooking now is easier. You can make many foods at the same time.

Grammar

The **verb** <u>is</u> tells about one thing.

Your Turn

COLLABORATE

Based on "Life at Home," do you think home life is better now, or was it better in the past? Why?

Go Digital!
Write your response online.
Use your editing checklist.

North Wind Picture Archives

L.1.1e See the California Standards section.

87

Essential Question
How do we get our food?

Go Digital!

©Roland Weihrauch/dpa/Corbis

SL.1.1a See the California Standards section.

Food's Journey

Talk About It

What happens to farm goods before you eat them?

after

Bread has a crust **after** it is baked.

buy

They **buy** oranges at the store.

done

They are **done** and ready to eat.

RF.1.3b, RF.1.3g See the California Standards section.

every

Every grape is plump and purple.

soon

They will go to the store **soon**.

work

Machines help do the **work**.

Your Turn

COLLABORATE

Say the sentence for each word. Then make up another sentence.

Go Digital! Use the online visual glossary

oo, u

The letters oo and u can make the sound you hear in the middle of **good** and **push**.

cook	looking	pull
hood	foot	took
hooked	books	wool
put	stood	shook

Holli Conger

92   RF.1.3b, RF.1.3f See the California Standards section.

Jake put on his wool coat.

He will pull up the hood.

COLLABORATE

Your Turn

Look for these words with oo and u in "A Look at Breakfast."

look	good	put
full	cooked	pulled

Essential Question

How do we get our food?

Read about where breakfast foods come from.

Go Digital!

A Look at Breakfast

Bread is good for breakfast. But this isn't bread yet. It is wheat. Flour will be made from the wheat.

The wheat is crushed to make flour.

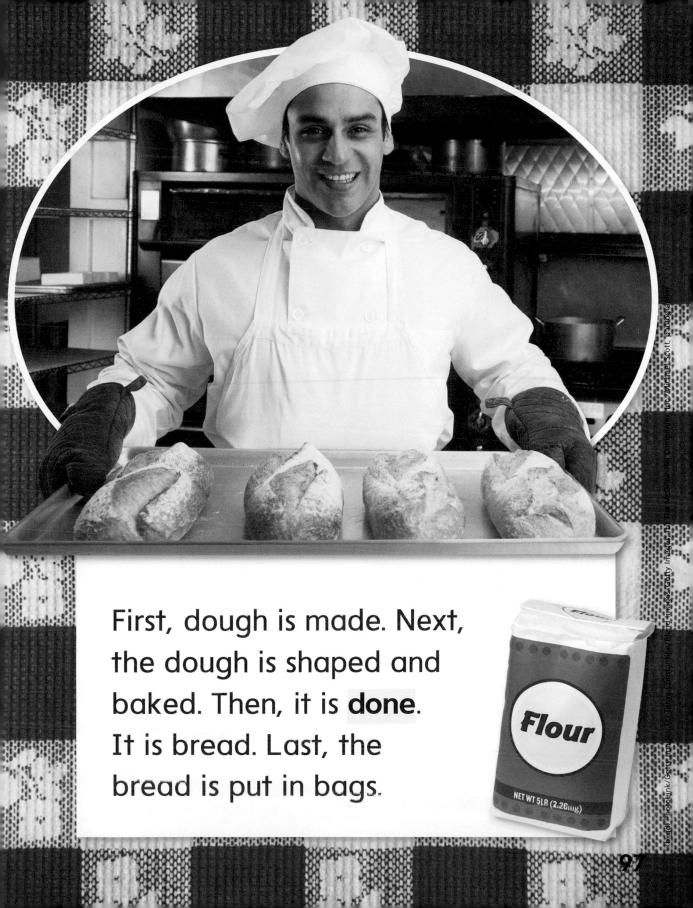

First, dough is made. Next, the dough is shaped and baked. Then, it is **done**. It is bread. Last, the bread is put in bags.

Grape jam is good on bread. But this isn't jam yet. It is a grape vine full of grapes.

Grapes grow on vines and then are picked when they are ripe.

Trucks take the grapes to a plant.
Every grape is crushed to make
mush. **After** that, the mush
is cooked. Now, it is
grape jam. Yum!

Orange juice is good for breakfast, too! Lots and lots of sun makes oranges big and ripe. They will taste good. **Soon**, the big, ripe oranges will get pulled down.

Trucks take piles and piles of oranges to a plant. Then, they get washed. Next, they get crushed. Big sacks get filled with juice.

The food is shipped in trucks to shops. It is stacked up. Now, it is for sale. People will **buy** it and bring it home. It will make a good breakfast!

It takes **work** to make food
for breakfast.

Food	Where It Comes From	How It Is Made
bread	wheat	Wheat is crushed into flour. Dough is made. Dough is baked into bread.
grape jam	grapes	Grapes are crushed to make mush. Mush is cooked into jam.
orange juice	oranges	Oranges are crushed into juice.

Sequence

Authors often give information in **sequence**, or time order. Words such as **first, next, then,** and **last** help you understand the sequence.

 Find Text Evidence

Find the first thing that happens when flour is made into bread.

page 97

First, dough is made. Next, the dough is shaped and baked. Then, it is **done**. It is bread. Last, the bread is put in bags.

First

Dough is made.

Next

The dough is shaped and baked.

Then

It is done.

Last

The bread is put in bags.

Your Turn

Talk about how other foods in "A Look at Breakfast" are made. Tell what happens in sequence.

Go Digital! *Use the interactive graphic organizer*

D. Hurst/A.amy

Pages 94–103

Write About the Text

Lisa

I answered the question: **Which breakfast item do you think is the hardest to make? Why?**

Student Model: *Opinion*

Reasons
I gave a reason for my opinion.

I think bread is the hardest breakfast food to make. It takes many steps to make it.

First, the farmer grows wheat. Then, wheat is crushed into flour.

W.1.1 See the California Standards section.

Facts
I used facts from the selection to support my opinion.

Next, the flour is mixed to make dough. Last, the dough is shaped into loaves and baked.

It takes more steps to make bread than jam or juice. It isn't easy to make bread.

Grammar

The **contraction** **isn't** is a short way of writing the words is and not.

COLLABORATE

Your Turn

Choose one set of pages. Would you rather have the original item or the finished product for breakfast?

Go Digital!
Write your response online.
Use your editing checklist.

California Common Core State Standards

At the bottom of some pages in this book, you will see letters and numbers. What do these numbers and letters mean? In **RL.1.1**, **RL** stands for **R**eading **S**tandards for **L**iterature. The number **1** stands for Grade 1. The number **1** is the standard number.

Subject Area	Grade Level	Standard Number
RL	1	1

This California standard is about being able to ask questions and give answers based on information in the text to show what you have learned.

1. Ask and answer such questions as *who, what, where, when, why,* and *how* to demonstrate understanding of key details in a text.

This means that you will learn to ask questions to find out the information you need from a story. You will learn to understand what the author says directly in the text. You will also learn to find deeper meaning in the text by using details and clues. The author put these clues into the story. It is the reader's job to figure them out!

The Grade 1 California Standards for Reading and Language Arts have six subject areas.

RL = Reading Standards for Literature

RI = Reading Standards for Informational Text

RF = Reading Standards for Foundational Skills

W = Writing Standards

SL = Speaking and Listening Standards

L = Language Standards

Your standards in all of these subject areas follow. **Take a look!**

English Language Arts & Literacy in History/ Social Studies, Science, and Technical Subjects

Grade 1

Reading Standards for Literature	
Key Ideas and Details	
RL.1.1	Ask and answer questions about key details in a text.
RL.1.2	Retell stories, including key details, and demonstrate understanding of their central message or lesson.
RL.1.3	Describe characters, settings, and major events in a story, using key details.
Craft and Structure	
RL.1.4	Identify words and phrases in stories or poems that suggest feelings or appeal to the senses. (See grade 1 Language standards 4–6 for additional expectations.) CA
RL.1.5	Explain major differences between books that tell stories and books that give information, drawing on a wide reading of a range of text types.
RL.1.6	Identify who is telling the story at various points in a text.
Integration of Knowledge and Ideas	
RL.1.7	Use illustrations and details in a story to describe its characters, setting, or events.
RL.1.8	(Not applicable to literature)
RL.1.9	Compare and contrast the adventures and experiences of characters in stories.
Range of Reading and Level of Text Complexity	
RL.1.10	With prompting and support, read prose and poetry of appropriate complexity for grade 1.
RL.1.10a	Activate prior knowledge related to the information and events in a text. CA
RL.1.10b	Confirm predictions about what will happen next in a text. CA

Reading Standards for Informational Text

Key Ideas and Details

RI.1.1	Ask and answer questions about key details in a text.
RI.1.2	Identify the main topic and retell key details of a text.
RI.1.3	Describe the connection between two individuals, events, ideas, or pieces of information in a text.

Craft and Structure

RI.1.4	Ask and answer questions to help determine or clarify the meaning of words and phrases in a text. (See grade 1 Language standards 4–6 for additional expectations.) CA
RI.1.5	Know and use various text structures (e.g., sequence) and text features (e.g., headings, tables of contents, glossaries, electronic menus, icons) to locate key facts or information in a text. CA
RI.1.6	Distinguish between information provided by pictures or other illustrations and information provided by the words in a text.

Integration of Knowledge and Ideas

RI.1.7	Use the illustrations and details in a text to describe its key ideas.
RI.1.8	Identify the reasons an author gives to support points in a text.
RI.1.9	Identify basic similarities in and differences between two texts on the same topic (e.g., in illustrations, descriptions, or procedures).

Range of Reading and Level of Text Complexity

RI.1.10	With prompting and support, read informational texts appropriately complex for grade 1.
RI.1.10a	Activate prior knowledge related to the information and events in a text. CA
RI.1.10b	Confirm predictions about what will happen next in a text. CA

Grade 1

Reading Standards for Foundational Skills

Print Concepts

RF.1.1	Demonstrate understanding of the organization and basic features of print.
RF.1.1a	Recognize the distinguishing features of a sentence (e.g., first word, capitalization, ending punctuation).

Phonological Awareness

RF.1.2	Demonstrate understanding of spoken words, syllables, and sounds (phonemes).
RF.1.2a	Distinguish long from short vowel sounds in spoken single-syllable words.
RF.1.2b	Orally produce single-syllable words by blending sounds (phonemes), including consonant blends.
RF.1.2c	Isolate and pronounce initial, medial vowel, and final sounds (phonemes) in spoken single-syllable words.
RF.1.2d	Segment spoken single-syllable words into their complete sequence of individual sounds (phonemes).

Phonics and Word Recognition

RF.1.3	Know and apply grade-level phonics and word analysis skills in decoding words both in isolation and in text. CA
RF.1.3a	Know the spelling-sound correspondences for common consonant digraphs.
RF.1.3b	Decode regularly spelled one-syllable words.
RF.1.3c	Know final -e and common vowel team conventions for representing long vowel sounds.
RF.1.3d	Use knowledge that every syllable must have a vowel sound to determine the number of syllables in a printed word.
RF.1.3e	Decode two-syllable words following basic patterns by breaking the words into syllables.
RF.1.3f	Read words with inflectional endings.
RF.1.3g	Recognize and read grade-appropriate irregularly spelled words.

Fluency	
RF.1.4	Read with sufficient accuracy and fluency to support comprehension.
RF.1.4a	Read on-level text with purpose and understanding.
RF.1.4b	Read on-level text orally with accuracy, appropriate rate, and expression on successive readings.
RF.1.4c	Use context to confirm or self-correct word recognition and understanding, rereading as necessary.

Writing Standards

Text Types and Purposes

W.1.1	Write opinion pieces in which they introduce the topic or name the book they are writing about, state an opinion, supply a reason for the opinion, and provide some sense of closure.
W.1.2	Write informative/explanatory texts in which they name a topic, supply some facts about the topic, and provide some sense of closure.
W.1.3	Write narratives in which they recount two or more appropriately sequenced events, include some details regarding what happened, use temporal words to signal event order, and provide some sense of closure.

Production and Distribution of Writing

W.1.4	(Begins in grade 2) CA
W.1.5	With guidance and support from adults, focus on a topic, respond to questions and suggestions from peers, and add details to strengthen writing as needed.
W.1.6	With guidance and support from adults, use a variety of digital tools to produce and publish writing, including in collaboration with peers.

Research to Build and Present Knowledge

W.1.7	Participate in shared research and writing projects (e.g., explore a number of "how-to" books on a given topic and use them to write a sequence of instructions).
W.1.8	With guidance and support from adults, recall information from experiences or gather information from provided sources to answer a question.
W.1.9	(Begins in grade 4)

Range of Writing

W.1.10	(Begins in grade 2) CA

Speaking and Listening Standards

Comprehension and Collaboration

SL.1.1   Participate in collaborative conversations with diverse partners about *grade 1 topics and texts* with peers and adults in small and larger groups.

SL.1.1a   Follow agreed-upon rules for discussions (e.g., listening to others with care, speaking one at a time about the topics and texts under discussion).

SL.1.1b   Build on others' talk in conversations by responding to the comments of others through multiple exchanges.

SL.1.1c   Ask questions to clear up any confusion about the topics and texts under discussion.

SL.1.2   Ask and answer questions about key details in a text read aloud or information presented orally or through other media.

SL.1.2a   Give, restate, and follow simple two-step directions. CA

SL.1.3   Ask and answer questions about what a speaker says in order to gather additional information or clarify something that is not understood.

Presentation of Knowledge and Ideas

SL.1.4   Describe people, places, things, and events with relevant details, expressing ideas and feelings clearly.

SL.1.4a   Memorize and recite poems, rhymes, and songs with expression. CA

SL.1.5   Add drawings or other visual displays to descriptions when appropriate to clarify ideas, thoughts, and feelings.

SL.1.6   Produce complete sentences when appropriate to task and situation. (See grade 1 Language standards 1 and 3 for specific expectations.)

Language Standards

Conventions of Standard English

L.1.1	Demonstrate command of the conventions of standard English grammar and usage when writing or speaking.
L.1.1a	Print all upper- and lowercase letters.
L.1.1b	Use common, proper, and possessive nouns.
L.1.1c	Use singular and plural nouns with matching verbs in basic sentences (e.g., *He hops; We hop*).
L.1.1d	Use personal (subject, object), possessive, and indefinite pronouns (e.g., *I, me, my; they, them, their; anyone, everything*). CA
L.1.1e	Use verbs to convey a sense of past, present, and future (e.g., *Yesterday I walked home; Today I walk home; Tomorrow I will walk home*).
L.1.1f	Use frequently occurring adjectives.
L.1.1g	Use frequently occurring conjunctions (e.g., *and, but, or, so, because*).
L.1.1h	Use determiners (e.g., articles, demonstratives).
L.1.1i	Use frequently occurring prepositions (e.g., *during, beyond, toward*).
L.1.1j	Produce and expand complete simple and compound declarative, interrogative, imperative, and exclamatory sentences in response to prompts.
L.1.2	Demonstrate command of the conventions of standard English capitalization, punctuation, and spelling when writing.
L.1.2a	Capitalize dates and names of people.
L.1.2b	Use end punctuation for sentences.
L.1.2c	Use commas in dates and to separate single words in a series.
L.1.2d	Use conventional spelling for words with common spelling patterns and for frequently occurring irregular words.
L.1.2e	Spell untaught words phonetically, drawing on phonemic awareness and spelling conventions.

Knowledge of Language

L.1.3	(Begins in grade 2)

Grade 1 · Language Standards (continued)

Vocabulary Acquisition and Use

L.1.4	Determine or clarify the meaning of unknown and multiple-meaning words and phrases based on *grade 1 reading and content,* choosing flexibly from an array of strategies.
L.1.4a	Use sentence-level context as a clue to the meaning of a word or phrase.
L.1.4b	Use frequently occurring affixes as a clue to the meaning of a word.
L.1.4c	Identify frequently occurring root words (e.g., *look*) and their inflectional forms (e.g., *looks, looked, looking*).
L.1.5	With guidance and support from adults, demonstrate understanding of word relationships and nuances in word meanings.
L.1.5a	Sort words into categories (e.g., colors, clothing) to gain a sense of the concepts the categories represent.
L.1.5b	Define words by category and by one or more key attributes (e.g., a *duck* is a bird that swims; a *tiger* is a large cat with stripes).
L.1.5c	Identify real-life connections between words and their use (e.g., note places at home that are *cozy*).
L.1.5d	Distinguish shades of meaning among verbs differing in manner (e.g., *look, peek, glance, stare, glare, scowl*) and adjectives differing in intensity (e.g., *large, gigantic*) by defining or choosing them or by acting out the meanings.
L.1.6	Use words and phrases acquired through conversations, reading and being read to, and responding to texts, including using frequently occurring conjunctions to signal simple relationships (e.g., *because*).